MYTHOLOGY DICTIONARY

Title: Mythology Dictionary

ISBN-13: 978-1-942825-17-3

Author: Kambiz Mostofizadeh

Publisher: Mikazuki Publishing House™ (U.S.P.T.O. Serial Number 85705702)

Description: Mythology Dictionary gives you the A to Z of myths and folklore from various cultures around the world.

I0102135

MYTHOLOGY DICTIONARY

Myths and folklore are prominent in every culture on earth and every culture features unique heroes, deities, and figures that they feel are important for veneration. This book is by no means an all-inclusive dictionary of characters in mythology, it is however an amalgamation of the characters that are noteworthy for listing. There may be characters missing but that is what 2nd editions are for. The myth of the Dragon, for example, is a myth that is nearly universal. Every culture contains some kind of mythical bird with supernatural abilities. Every culture contains a story about a flood. What is unique about the Dragon myth is the distance between cultures

MYTHOLOGY DICTIONARY

that experienced it. Either ancient cultures were communicating or they shared a common heritage. Common myths and folklore permeate popular culture and their heritage has been maintained through the diligent writing and researching of writers and scholars alike. Myths live on forever because they contain ideals and values that are universal to all humankind. Hercules passing great obstacles is the representation of humankind's passing of great obstacles. Humans share myths because they share ideals and values, and that is why the myths continue to be shared, generation to generation. Certain myths, like myths about Aliens, Zombies, or

MYTHOLOGY DICTIONARY

Vampires, continue through their inclusion in movies and fictional books. Popular TV shows focused around zombies are applauded because myths are symbols. Zombies, as a symbol, represent the modern human being trapped in over-crowded areas with an excess density of people. What are the main characters in a zombie movie doing? Escaping from zombies. What does the modern 9-5 type human wish more than anything? To leave the mass of people surrounding him/her and head to the outdoors for peace, quiet, and fresh air. Myths symbolize humanity's struggle against the odds, whether they be natural or supernatural. By reading about

MYTHOLOGY DICTIONARY

myths, legends, and folklore, we learn more about the difficulties that these characters undergo, giving us lessons that we may use for ourselves. Each character stands to teach us something through the course of their adventure, and each of their stories were precisely written to convey a message to the listener or reader. The message could be, for example, what to avoid and what actions not to take, as in the case of a fable. The message could also be about life, attempting to give us deeper insight in to our own lives.

A

Abominable Snowman – Legend of a Sasquatch like creature that lives in mountainous areas.

Achelous - The son of Oceanus and Tethys. He contended with Hercules and was defeated. After his defeat he was changed into a river.

Acheron - A river that is fabled as one of the rivers of hell.

Achilles - The son of Peleus and Thetis, and the bravest of all the

Greeks in the Trojan war. During his infancy his mother dipped him into the river Styx, which rendered him invulnerable in every part except the heel, by which she held him. It is said that Paris aimed an arrow at his vulnerable heel, in the tenth year of the Trojan war, of which wound he died.

Acis - A shepherd of Sicily. Polyphemus, king of the Cyclops of Sicily, crushed him to death through jealousy. The Deities changed Acis into a stream, which rises from mount Aetna.

Aconteous - A famous hunter, changed into a stone by the head of Medusa.

Actaeon - A famous huntsman, son of Aristasus and Autonoe. He was changed by Diana into a stag and devoured by his own dogs.

Actis - Son of Sol. He went from Greece into Egypt, where he taught astrology and founded Heliopolis.

MYTHOLOGY DICTIONARY

Adamantaea - Jupiter's nurse in Crete. To protect him from his father Saturn, who intended to have devoured him, she suspended him in his cradle to a tree, that he might be found neither on earth, the sea, nor in heaven. To drown his cries she caused the Corybantes to sound drums and other musical instruments around the tree.

Admetus - King of Pherae in Thessaly. Apollo, when banished from heaven, is said to have tended his flocks for nine years, and to have obtained that Admetus should never die provided another person laid down his life for him; a proof of affection which his wife Alceste cheerfully gave him.

Adonis - Son of Cinyras, a rich king of Cyprus. He was often cautioned by Venus not to hunt wild beasts, an amusement in which he much delighted. He slighted the advice of the Deity, and at last received a mortal bite from a wild boar. Venus, after shedding many tears at his death, changed him into the flower called anemony.

MYTHOLOGY DICTIONARY

Aea - A huntress changed into an island by the Deities, to rescue her from the pursuit of the river Phasis.

Aegis - The shield of Jupiter, covered with the skin of the goat Amalthaea. Jupiter gave this shield to Minerva, who placed upon it, as a boss, the head of Medusa.

Aeneas - Son of Anchises and Venus. He married Creusa, daughter of Priam, king of Troy. During the

MYTHOLOGY DICTIONARY

Trojan war he behaved with great valor. From him Romulus is supposed to have derived his descent.

Aeolus - The king of storms and winds. He gave Ulysses a bag containing all the winds that could blow against his vessel when he returned to Ithaca. The companions of Ulysses contrived to untie the bag and set the winds at liberty, which caused his disastrous voyage.

Aesculapius - Son of Apollo, and the Deity of medicine. He restored many to life, of which Pluto complained to Jupiter, who struck Aesculapius with thunder, but Apollo, angry at the death of his son, killed the Cyclops who forged the thunder-bolts.

Afterlife – The belief that the spirit of the body continues life after death.

Alcyone or Halcyone - Daughter of Aeolus. Her husband was Ceyx, who was drowned as he was going to Claros. The Deities apprised Alcyone of her husband's fate in a dream, and when on the morrow she found his body washed on the sea-shore, she threw herself into the sea, and was with her husband changed into birds of the same name, which keep the water calm while they build, and sit on their nests, on the surface of the sea.

Alcyoneus - A giant killed by Hercules. His daughters mourning his death, threw themselves into the sea, and were changed by Amphitrite into Alcyones.

Alien – An extraterrestrial being that is not from the planet earth.

Aloeus – A giant. Son of Terra and Titan.

Amalthea – Daughter of Melissus, King of Crete, who fed Jupiter with goat's milk; hence some Authors have called her a goat.

Amaterasu – Sun deity in Japanese mythology.

Ambisagrus – French deity of thunder.

Ambrosia - Festivals in honor of Bacchus, in some cities of Greece. They were the same as the Brumalia of the Romans. The food of the deities was called Ambrosia. The word signifies immortal.

Ameles - A river of hell, whose waters no vessel could contain.

Ammon - A name of Jupiter, worshipped in Libya.

Ambarvalia - A joyful procession round the ploughed fields, in honor of Ceres. A sow, a sheep, and a bull, were always immolated on the occasion.

Amphitrite - Daughter of Oceanus and Tethys, and wife of Neptune.

Amun – Egyptian deity of air.

Anchises - The father of Aeneas.

Ancile - A sacred shield which fell from heaven in the reign of Numa. Upon the preservation of this shield depended the fate of the Roman Empire.

Andromache - Daughter of Eetion, king of Thebes in Cilicia, married to Hector, son of Priam, king of Troy.

Anna – A deity in whose honor the Romans instituted festivals. She is supposed to be the sister of Dido,

who fled from Carthage and came to
Italy, where she was honorably
treated by Aeneas.

Antaeus - A giant of Libya, son of
Terra and Neptune. Hercules
attacked him, but as he received
new strength from his mother as
often as he touched the ground,
Hercules lifted him up in the air and
squeezed him to death in his arms.

Anthesteria - Festivals in honor of
Bacchus among the Greeks.

Anubis - Egyptian deity whose
worship was also introduced into
Greece and Italy. He is supposed to
be the Mercury of the Greeks.

MYTHOLOGY DICTIONARY

Apollo - The son of Jupiter and Latona, called also Phoebus, or the sun. He was the deity, according to the ancients, who inflicted plagues on mankind, and at that time always appeared surrounded with clouds. His most famous oracles were at Delphi, Delos, Glares, Tenedos, Cyrrha, and Patara.

Arachne - A woman of Colophon, daughter of a dyer. She challenged Minerva to a trial of skill in the art of needle-work. Being defeated by the deity, she hung herself in despair, but was immediately afterwards turned into a spider by her successful competitor.

Ares – Deity of War. Worshipped by Greeks.

Argus - The son of Arestor, who had one hundred eyes, of which only two were asleep at the same time : for this cause he was employed by Juno to watch Io ; but Mercury, by the command of Jupiter, having lulled all his eyes to sleep by the sound of his lyre, slew him. Juno placed the eyes of Argus on the tail of the peacock, a bird sacred to her divinity.

Artemis – Greek Deity. Patron of Animals.

Arthur – Also known as King Arthur. Son of British King Uther Pendragon, was raised by Merlin the Druid. Arthur was Sarmatian (an Iranian tribe that settled in Eastern Europe) as were many of his Knights. Arthur became King after pulling Excalibur from the stone in which it was lodged in.

Asklepios – Deity of healing and medicine, worshipped by Greeks.

Astral Projection – An experience that involves your spirit leaving your body and travelling to an astral plane.

Astarte – Greek version of Ishtar. Worshipped as a symbol of female divinity.

Astrea - Daughter of Titanus (Saturn's brother) and Aurora. She was called Justice, of which virtue she was the Deity. She lived upon earth during the golden age, but the wickedness and impiety of the brazen and iron ages drove her to heaven. She was placed among the constellations of the zodiac, under the name of Virgo.

Astreus - One of the Titans who made war against Jupiter.

Astrology – Fortune-telling method that uses the stars to predict the future.

Atalanta - A daughter of Schaeneus king of Scyros. Remarkable for her swiftness in running. Having promised to marry the man who could reach the goal first in a race with herself, many offered to compete with her in running : she, however, defeated them all, until Hippomanes presented himself. Venus had presented him with three golden apples from the garden of the Hesperides ; and as soon as he had started in the course he artfully threw down the apples at some distance one from the other. While Atalanta, charmed with the apples, stopped to pick them up, Hippomanes hastened to the goal, and obtained Atalanta in marriage.

Ate - A daughter of Jupiter: she was the Deity of all evil. She raised such jealousy and discord among the Deities that her father dragged her away from heaven by the hair of her head, and banished her to earth, where she immediately incited mankind to wickedness^ and stirred up continual commotions.

Athena – Greek deity of war.

Atlantides - The seven daughters of Atlas: their names were Maia, Electra, Taygeta, Asterope, Merope, Alcyone, and Celaeno. They make that constellation in the heavens called the Pleiades.

Atlantis – Legendary island that was thought to exist in ancient times, with access to technology and advanced tools. Its location is widely disputed.

Atlas - One of the Titans, son of Japetus and Clymene, one of the Oceanides. He studied astronomy, and from the circumstance of his frequenting elevated places, the better to observe the heavenly bodies, arose the fable of his supporting the heavens on his back, or, as others say. Atlas was changed into a mountain in Africa, which is so high that the ancients imagined the heavens rested on its top.

Augeas - The son of Elius. He was one of the Argonauts, and afterwards ascended the throne of Elis. The stables in which he kept an immense number of oxen and goats had never been cleaned so that the task seemed an impossibility; nevertheless, Hercules undertook it, upon condition that he should receive as his reward a tenth part of the king's herds. He effected tie task, by turning the course of the river Alpheus, or, as some say, the Peneus, which immediately carried away the filth. The proverb of the Augean stable is now applied to an impossibility.

Aurora - The reputed daughter of Titan and Terra. She is represented by the poets as drawn in a rose-colored chariot by the Horse, and opening with her rosy fingers the gates of the east. Nox and Somnus fly before her, and the stars of heaven disappear at her approach. She always precedes the sun, and is the harbinger of his approach.

Automatic Writing – Method used by spiritualists to communicate with the dead. Involves the use of a planchette with a pencil inserted in it to allow for the writing of messages by spirits.

Avernus - A lake of Campania, whose waters were so putrid that no birds were ever seen on its banks. The ancients called it the entrance of hell.

B

Bacchanalia - Feasts in honor of Bacchus at Rome, the same as the Dionysia of the Greeks.

Bacchus - The son of Jupiter and Semele. Silenus was his foster-father. He subdued the east, penetrating beyond those regions, which were afterwards conquered by Alexander the Great. The people easily submitted to him, and gratefully elevated to the rank of a Deity, the hero who taught them the use of the vine, the cultivation of the earth, and the manner of making honey. His army consisted as well of women as of men, all inspired with divine fury, and armed with thursi, cymbals, etc. Bacchus is the Osiris of the Egyptians, and his history is drawn from the Egyptian traditions concerning that ancient king.

Bacchus is styled the Deity of Wine, and his festivals were celebrated under circumstances of great licentiousness, his followers, dressed as satyrs, being at those times constantly intoxicated. In Greece Bacchus was called Dionysius.

Baosheng Dadi – Chinese deity of medicine.

Basilea - A daughter of Coelus and Terra.

Bastet – Egyptian deity of music and dance.

Baubo – A woman who entertained Ceres, when she was engaged in her search all over the world for her

daughter Proserpine, whom Pluto
had carried to hell and married.

Baucis - An old woman, who, with
her husband Philemon, entertained
to the best of their ability Jupiter and
Mercury, when they were travelling
In disguise over Asia. As a reward
for their hospitality, Jupiter
metamorphosed their poor cottage
into a magnificent temple, of which
they were made priest and priestess.
The Deity like-wise conceded to
them their wish to die
contemporaneously. After their death
they were changed into two trees

which adorned the entrance to their temple.

Belenus - A divinity of the Gauls; the same as the Apollo of the Greeks and the Orus of the Egyptians.

Bellona - The Deity of war, and the sister of Mars, whose chariot she prepared when he was going to war: she always herself appeared in battle, armed with a whip, her hair disheveled, and a torch in her hand.

Belus - One of the most ancient kings of Babylon, worshipped as a Deity after his death with much ceremony, by the Assyrians and Babylonians. The temple of Belus was the most ancient and the most magnificent temple in the world. It was originally the tower of Babel.

Bigfoot – Also known as the Sasquatch. A human like creature with ape like qualities. Bipedal and extremely powerful. Famous in American folklore.

Bishamon – Japanese deity of war.

MYTHOLOGY DICTIONARY

Bona Dea – A name given by the Greeks to Ops, Vesta, and Cybele; by the Romans to Fauna or Fatua. The festivals of this Deity were celebrated only in the nighty by the Roman matrons, in the houses of the highest officers of the state.

Boogeyman – Urban legend prominent in Western culture about a monster that lives in closets and targets children.

Bola de Fuego – Colombia myth about a woman that turned in to a ball of flames from anger and is seen rolling through Colombia in the shape of a ball of flames.

Boreas - The name of the north wind, blowing from the Hyperborean mountains. Boreas was the son of Astreus and Aurora.

Brachmanes - Indian philosophers, who devoted themselves wholly to the worship of the Deities. They believed that Brahma, their chief deity, created as many worlds as there are parts in the body, which they reckoned fourteen. They also believed that there were seven seas; one of water, one of milk, one of curds, one of butter, one of salt, one of sugar, and one of wine, each blessed with its particular paradise. The Brachmans were accustomed to endure labors and live with frugality and abstinence for thirty-seven years; after which time, they were permitted to indulge themselves in all licentious pleasures, without control.

Briareus - A famous giant, son of Coelos and Terca, who had fifty heads and one hundred hands. When Juno, Minerva, and Neptune tried to dethrone Jupiter, Briareus ascended to heaven, and seating himself, so terrified the conspirators by his fierce looks, that they gave up their plan. He also assisted the giants in their war against the Deities. Ultimately he was cast under mount Aetna, where his groans continue to be heard.

Brumalia - Feasts at Rome in honor of Bacchus.

Bunyan, Paul – Giant lumberjack famous in American folklore. He is accompanied by Babe the Blue Ox who has supernatural-like strength. Was made famous by oral storytelling by loggers.

C

Cacub - A famous robber, whom Hercules squeezed and strangled, although he was a three-headed monster constantly vomiting fire.

Caduceus - The rod Rome by Mercury, which was entwined by two serpents. With it, Mercury conducted the souls of the dead to the infernal regions, lulled to sleep, and even raised the dead to life.

Caeculus - A son of Vulcan; so called from the smallness of his eyes.

Cai Shen – Chinese deity of prosperity.

Cailleach – Female deity with the ability to control forces of nature. Responsible for creation of hills and mountains.

MYTHOLOGY DICTIONARY

Calliope - One of the nine Muses, daughter of Jupiter and Mnemosyne. She presided over eloquence and heroic poetry. She was generally represented with a trumpet in her right hand, and in her left the three most famous epic poems of antiquity.

Calypso - One of the Oceanides, who reigned in the island of Ogygia. Ulysses was shipwrecked on her coasts, and there detained by the Deity for seven years.

Camelot – City were King Arthur reigned and held court.

Candileja – Ghost light phenomenon over bodies of water in Colombian folklore.

Candle – Paraffin object that emits light from a wick powered flame. Used by witches to amplify or increase the power of their spells.

Castor and Pollux - Twin brothers, sons of Jupiter and Leda. They make the constellations in the heavens called Gemini, which never appear together, but when one rises the other sets, and so on alternately.

Celaeno - One of the Harpies.

Centauri - A people of Thessaly, half men and half horses. Their ignorant neighbors supposed them to form a part of the animals they were riding. The most celebrated of the centaurs

MYTHOLOGY DICTIONARY

were Chiron, Eurytus, Amycus,
Gryneus, Caumas, Lycidas, Arneus,
Medon, Rhoetus, Pisenor,
Mermeros, and Pholus.

Centeotl – The deity of maize (corn)
in Aztec folklore. Maize was highly
important to ancient Aztec civilization
and the farming of corn was carried
out with paying reverence to
Centeotl as well as other deities.
Centeotl was usually represented
In the form of a young male. He is
said to have been born on the day
sign 1 Xochitl.

Cerberus - Pluto's dog which
guarded the entrance to hell. He is
represented with three heads.

Cerealia - Festivals in honor of
Ceres.

Ceres - The Deity of corn and
harvests, daughter of Saturn and
Vesta. She taught mankind to
plough, sow, and reap com, to make
bread, etc. Sicily was supposed to
be the favorite retreat of this Deity.
The Romans paid her great
adoration, and her festivals were

held by the Roman matrons during eight days in the month of April. These matrons always bore lighted torches, in commemoration of Ceres search for her daughter Proserpine, who had been carried off by Pluto.

Cernunnos – French deity of agriculture.

Ceto - A daughter of Pectus and Terra. She was the mother of the Gorgons.

Ceyx - A king of Trachinia, son of Lucifer, and husband of Alcyone.

Chac – Mayan deity of rain and lightning.

CERES.

Chalchiuhtlicue – She was the Aztec deity of rivers and lakes.

Chang'e – Chinese deity of the moon.

Chaos - A rude and shapeless mass of matter, which, according to the poets, pre-existed the formation of the world. Chaos was deemed as

one of the oldest of the Deities and
invoked as one of the infernal
deities.

Charities - The Graces, daughters
of Jupiter and Venus. Their names
were Aglaia, Thalia, & Euphrosyne.
They are represented as three
modest and beautiful young women,
who presided over kindness and all
good offices.

Charon - A Deity of hell, son of
Erebus and Nox, who conducted the
souls of the dead in a boat over the
rivers Styx and Acheron to the
infernal regions. As the dead had to
pay for their admission, it was
customary among the ancients to
place a piece of money under the
tongue of the defunct for Charon.

Charybdis – A whirlpool personified
as a woman; it was on the coast of
Sicily, opposite another whirlpool
called Scylla, which was on the coast
of Italy. These whirlpools were
formerly dangerous to sailors, now
from the improvements in navigation
of no consequence. "Incidit in
Scyllam, qui vult vitare Charybdim"

MYTHOLOGY DICTIONARY

became a proverb among the ancients.

Chenghuangshen – City deity in Chinese folklore.

Chimera - A monster with three heads continually vomiting flames. The foreparts of its body were those of a lion, the middle of a goat, and the hinder parts those of a dragon. The three heads respectively corresponded with each of these animals.

Chiron - The centaur who instructed Achilles, Aesculapius, Hercules, Jason, Peleus, and Aeneas in all the polite arts. He was placed by Jupiter (who at his own intercession deprived him of immortality) among the constellations, under the name of Sagittarius.

Chmun – Egyptian deity of water.

MYTHOLOGY DICTIONARY

Chons – Egyptian deity of the moon.

MYTHOLOGY DICTIONARY

Chupacabra – Blood sucking mythical creature that is popular in U.S. States like New Mexico. Known to feasts on goats and cattle.

Circe - A daughter of Sol and Perseis, celebrated for her knowledge of magic and poisonous herbs.

Cizin – Mayan deity of sacrifice.

Clio - One of the Muses. She presided over history.

Concordia - The Deity of peace, worshipped by the Romans.

Conjuring – Use of magic to affect the physical environment.

Consentes - A name given by the Romans to the twelve top deities; Jupiter, Mars, Mercury, Neptune, Vulcan, Apollo, Juno, Minerva, Ceres, Diana, Vesta, and Venus.

Coven – Group of witches or association of witches.

Cult – Unconventional veneration of an individual or item, organized as a group. Its qualities are dogmatic, rigid, extreme, and uniform.

Cupid - The son of Venus, and Deity of love. Among the ancients, he was worshipped with the same solemnities as his mother.

Curran – Pearl Curran was a woman that claimed to have authored a novel based on her experiences with a spirit.

Cybele - A daughter of Coelus and Terra, and wife of Saturn.

Cyclops - A race of giants, supposed to be sons of Coelus and Terra. They had but one eye in the middle of the forehead, which tradition arises from their custom of wearing small bucklers over their faces with an aperture in the middle, which corresponded exactly to the eye. They resided in Sicily, near mount Aetna, whence they have been supposed to be the workers of Vulcan, and to have fabricated the thunderbolts of Jupiter.

Cynthia - A surname of Diana, from Mount Cynthus, where she was bom.

Cynthius - A surname of Apollo from the same circumstance. The mountain was sacred to these twins.

MYTHOLOGY DICTIONARY

Cytherea - A surname of Venus from Cythera an island on the coast of Laconia sacred to her. Some suppose she rose from the sea near that island, others that she rose near Cyprus.

D

Demeter – Deity of the Harvest, worshipped by Greeks.

DIANA.

MYTHOLOGY DICTIONARY

Demon – An evil spirit.

Demonologist – Individual that specializes in the study of demons.

Destiny – The belief that a human's life is pre-determined.

Devil – Angel expelled from Heaven by God for refusing to bow down to human-kind. The Devil is represented in various forms; Snake, Hoofed horned Goat, etc. Featured in Abrahamic religions (Judaism, Christianity, Islam).

Diana - The Deity of hunting. Sixty of the Oceanides and twenty other nymphs were her attendants in the wood and forests she frequented. She as well as her brother Apollo had some oracles, among which those of Egypt, Cilicia, and Ephesus are the most known. Her name in the infernal regions was Hecate.

Dirae - The daughters of Acheron and Nox, who persecuted the souls of the wicked. They are supposed to be the same as the Furies, and

called Furies in hell, Harpies on
earth, and Dirae in heaven.

Cerberus

MYTHOLOGY DICTIONARY

Discordia - A malevolent deity, daughter of Nox, driven from heaven by Jupiter, for sowing dissension among the Deities. At the marriage of Peleus and Thetis, to which ceremony she had received no invitation, she threw an apple into the midst of the assembly with this inscription, "detur pulchriori". This apple produced much contention among the Deity, and infinite misfortunes to man. To it is ascribed the men of Troy, and the disasters the Greeks subsequently suffered.

Divination – Methods for forecasting the future; Oracles, Spirit Boards, Signs of nature, etc. Soothsayers would travel to towns offering their fortune-telling services.

Dragon – Legendary myth about a flying creature that is part snake, part bird, and part reptile. Symbols on ancient Chinese archeological sites show the oldest use of the Dragon. The Dragon is a water creature that is able to fly.

Dragon King – Chinese water deity.

Draugr – Mythical Norse zombie.

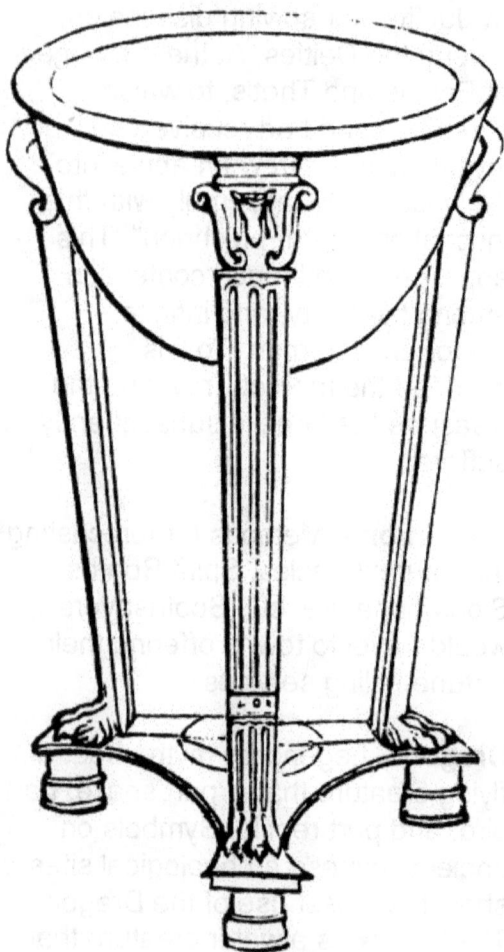

Oracle at Delphi

MYTHOLOGY DICTIONARY

Dream Walking – Supposed skill by witches that allows them to enter the dreams of anyone at will.

Druid - The ministers of religion among the ancient Gauls and Britons.

Dryades - Nymphs who presided over woods. They were not supposed to be immortal, but as genii whose lives were terminated with the tree over which they presided.

Dullahan – Headless horseman myth prominent in Irish folklore.

E

Each uisge – Mythical water creature in the shape of a horse, featured in Scottish mythology.

Echo - A daughter of Air and Tellus. She was deprived of the power of speech by Juno, excepting to answer questions which were put to her. She pined away and was afterwards changed into a stone which still retains the power of reflecting sound.

Ectoplasm – Liquid ejected from mediums during séance.

Eight Immortals – 8 mythical heroes in the pantheon of Chinese Taoist belief.

Egeria - A nymph of Aricia in Italy, by some supposed to be the same as Diana. She was the deity from whom Numa declared he received the wise laws he gave to the Romans, hoping by this means to sanctify them in the eyes of the people.

El Dorado – The city of Gold that was rumored to have been in North America or Central America. Many Native Americans were tortured and murdered by Spanish conquistadors looking to find the famed city.

Electra - One of the Oceanides, the wife of Atlas.

Eleusinia - A great festival held every fourth year by the Celeans, Lacedaemonians, and Cretans, and every fifth year by the Athenians, at Eleusis in Attica, in honor of Ceres and Proserpine. A mysterious secrecy was solemnly observed in the celebration of the ceremonies connected with this festival. None but the initiated were permitted to be present at its solemnities, all intruders being punished with death.

Eleutheria - A festival celebrated at Plataea in honor of Jupiter Eleutherius, as the assertor of liberty.

Elysium - An island in the infernal regions, where, according to the mythology of the ancients, the virtuous were placed after death. Here, happiness was complete, and all pleasures were innocent and refined. Authors vary as to the locality of the Elysian Fields, some saying that they were in the Fortunate islands, others in Italy; Lucian says they were supposed to be near the moon, and Plutarch in the center of the earth.

Endymion - A shepherd, son of Aethlius and Calyce, who required of

Jupiter that he might always be young, and to sleep as much as he wished. The fable of Endymion and Diana or the Moon, arises from his knowledge of astronomy, which led him to pass whole nights on the top of some high mountain.

Epimetheus - A son of one of the Ooeanides who married Pandora. He had the curiosity to open the box she brought with her, and from thence issued a train of evils, which from that moment has never ceased to afflict mankind. Hope only remained at the bottom, and she alone comforts men under misfortune. Epimetheus was afterwards changed into a monkey.

Erato - The muse who presides over lyric and amorous poetry.

Erebus - A deity of hell, the son of Chaos and Darkness. He personified Darkness, and is the father of Light and Day.

Eshu – Evil Spirit in Yoruba religion, practiced in Latin America and

Africa.

Eumenides - A name given to the Furies by the ancients. They sprang from the drops of blood which fell from the wound which Coelus received from his son Saturn. They received this name, which signifies benevolence, after they had ceased to persecute Orestes, who in gratitude erected a temple, and offered sacrifices to their divinity.

Europa - A daughter of Agenor, king of Phoenicia, carried by Jupiter in the form of a white bull to Crete, where she married Asterius, king of that island. She was the mother of Minos, Sarpedon, and Khadamanthus.

MYTHOLOGY DICTIONARY

Eurydome - One of the Oceanides, the mother of the Graces.

Euterpe - One of the Muses, daughter of Jupiter and Mnemosyne. She presided over music, and is regarded as the inventor of the flute and all wind instruments.

Excalibur Mythical sword of King Arthur.

F

Fama - The deity of report; She is always represented as blowing a trumpet.

Familiars – Pets, usually cats, under the control of witches.

Fangfeng – Chinese mythical character that saved the Chinese people during the Great Flood.

Fauna - A deity among the Romans. She was the wife of Faunus, and daughter of Picus.

Faunus - The son of a king of Italy who reigned 1300 years before

Christ. He was very hospitable to strangers. His great popularity, and his fondness for agriculture, made his subjects reyere him after his death as one of their country deities. He was represented with all the equipage of the satyrs.

Fauni - Rural deities, represented as having their legs, feet, and ears of goats, and the rest of the body human. They were called Satyrs by the Greeks.

Febalia - A festival in honor of the

dead at Rome, called also Februa; hence the name February. The oblations used in these sacrifices consisted of such provisions as the survivors could procure, and were placed on the graves of the deceased, whose manes were supposed to hover around and feast upon what had been procured for them by their friends. This festival lasted eleven days during which time the punishments in the infernal regions were supposed to be suspended and the manes to enjoy a brief space of rest and liberty.

Febonias – She was deity at Rome who presided over woods and groves.

Ferdowsi –Ferdowsi spent 30 years writing The Shahnama, which is focused on Iranian mythology and folklore.

Fidius Dius – An oath that Romans swore divinity to. Thought to be related to Jupiter, his cult was famous among farmers.

SEMONI SANCO
SANCTODEO FIDIO
SACRVM

DECVRIA SACERDO
BIDENTALIVM

Flora – She was the deity of flowers; represented as crowned with flowers, and holding in her hand the horn of plenty.

Floralia - Feasts in honor of Flora, at Rome.

Fortuna - The deity of Fortune, she is represented blindfolded, and holding a wheel in her hands, as an emblem of her inconsistency.

MYTHOLOGY DICTIONARY

G

Ganymedes – 1) A beautiful youth of Phrygia, taken to heaven by Jupiter and made cup-bearer to the Deities in the place of Hebe. 2) She was a deity that was better known by the name of Hebe.

Garuda – Large destructive mythical bird featured in Hindu mythology.

Genie – Elemental creature believed to be made of fire.

Ghost – Spirit or apparition.

Ghost Hunting – Finding spirits using audio and visual recording equipment.

Ghoul – Undead creature that roams at night, first featured in Iranian folklore.

Gigantes - The sons of Coelus and Terra. They were men of vast stature, and of proportional strength. They are often ignorantly confounded with the Titans, to

MYTHOLOGY DICTIONARY

whom they were nearly related. All the writers of antiquity, including Moses, support the existence of giants upon east Homer describes Tityus as covering nine acres when extended, and Plutarch mentions that when Sertorius opened the grave of Antaeus he found a skeleton which measured six cubits in length. The wars of the giants against Jupiter, like the wars of the Titans against Satarn, are much celebrated.

Gordius - A king of Phrygia, who tied the cords which attached his chariot to a pillar in the temple of Jupiter in so intricate a manner that the ends could not be seen. It having been reported that he, who could untie the Gordian knot should acquire the empire of Asia, Alexander the Great, to inspire his soldiers with courage, and his enemies with awe, cut the knot asunder with his sword.

Gorgones - Three sisters, daughters of Phorcys and Ceto; their names were Stheno, Euryale, and Medusa. Their hair was entwined with serpents, their body covered with impenetrable scales, and their teeth were as long as the tusks of a wild boar. Perseus slew the Gorgons, and presented the head of Medusa to Minerva, who placed it as a boss on her.

Great Flood – Universal legend about a flood that covered the earth in water for a period of time.

Griffon – Mythical creature that is a cross between an eagle and a lion, featured in Greek folklore. Originated in Iranian mythology.

Grimoire – Book of spells.

MYTHOLOGY DICTIONARY

Gringo Pela Cara – Myth about face peeling White people that kill local villagers in the Amazon jungle.

Guan Yu – Chinese deity of war.

Gyges - A Lydian who, according to Plato, descended into a chasm of the earth, where he found a brazen ring, which, when put on his finger, rendered him invisible. By means of the virtue of this ring he contrived to murder King Candaules, and usurp the sovereignty of Lydia.

H

Hamadryades - Nymphs who presided over trees, with which they were said to live and die.

Harpocrates - The Deity of silence. The Romans placed his statues at the entrance of their temples, to intimate that the mysteries of religion and of philosophy ought not to be revealed to the vulgar.

Harpyae - Three winged monsters with the faces of women, bodies of vultures, and hands and feet armed with claws. Their names were Aello, Celeno, and Ocypete.

Haunted – A place that is rumoured to have spirits within it.

Hebe – She was the Deity of youth, made cup-bearer to the Deities.

Hecate - Diana's appellation in hell; in heaven she was called Luna, as on earth Diana. Hence she is sometimes termed Diva triformis.

Heliades - The daughters of the Sun and Clymene. They were so afflicted at the death of their brother Phaeton, that the Deities changed them into poplars, and their tears into precious amber on the river Po.

Heracleia - A festival at Athens, ce-

lebrated every fifth year in honor of
Hercules.

Hercules - A celebrated hero,
ranked as a deity. He was the son of
Jupiter and Alcmena. Complying with
the commands of the oracle of
Apollo, he under-took to perform the
twelve labors imposed upon him by
Euryetheus, king of Argos and
Mycenae: whereof, the first was to
kill the Nemean lion, which ravaged
the country of Mycenae; the second
was to destroy the Lemsean hydra ;
the third, to catch alive and unhurt
the stag, famous for its swiftness, its
golden horns, and its brazen feet ;
the fourth, to capture a wild boar
which infested the neighborhood of
Erymanthus, committing dreadful
depredations; the fifth, to
cleanse the Augean stables ; the
sixth, to kill the carnivorous birds
which ravaged the country around
lake Stymphalis, in Arcadia ; the
seventh, to bring to Peloponnesus a
prodigious wild bull which laid waste
the island of Crete ; the eighth, to
obtain the mares of Diomedes, which
lived on human flesh ; the ninth, to
obtain the girdle of the queen of the

Amazons ; the tenth, to kill the monster Geryon; the eleventh, to gather and carry off the apples guarded by a dragon in the garden of the Hesperides ; and the twelfth to bring upon earth the three headed dog Cerberus which kept the gates of hell.

MYTHOLOGY DICTIONARY

Hermae - Statues of Mercury, in the city of Athens. Among the Greeks Mercury was called Hermes.

Hermione - A daughter of Mars and Venus, married to Cadmus. All the Deities, except Juno, honored her nuptials with their presence. Both she and Cadmus were changed into serpents and placed in the Elysian fields.

Hertha - A deity among the Germans, supposed to be the same as the earth.

Hesperides - Three nymphs, daughters of Hesperis and Atlas, appointed to guard the golden apples which Juno gave to Jupiter on the day of their marriage. The garden, in which the apples were kept, was carefully guarded by a dreadful dragon, which never slept. Hercules slew the dragon and carried off the apples.

Hecate

Hesperus - A name applied by the poets to the planet Venus, when she appears in the western sky, and shines after the sun has set.

Hesus - A deity among the French, with the same attributes as the Mars of the Romans.

Hombre Bufeo – Mythical pink dolphin that transforms in to a handsome man that impregnates women and disappears. Featured in Colombian mythology.

Hombre Caiman – Mythical half-alligator half-man that haunts waterways in Colombian folklore.

Horae - Three sisters, daughters of Jupiter; the same as the seasons who pre- sided over spring, summer, and winter, represented by the poets as opening the gates of heaven.

Hebe

MYTHOLOGY DICTIONARY

Horus - An Egyptian deity, the son of Osiris and Isis.

Houyi –Chinese deity of archery.

Hunab Ku – Mayan deity of creation.

Huracan – Mayan deity of storm.

Hyacinthus - The son of Amyclas and Diomede, killed by Zephyrus. Apollo was so disconsolate at his deaths that he changed his blood into the flower bearing his name, and placed his body among the constellations.

Hydra - A monster with a hundred heads (according to Diodorus). Hercules slew this monster, which had infested the neighborhood of lake Lema, in Peloponnesus. Juno, jealous of the glory Hercules was obtaining by this deed, sent a crab to bite his foot. Hercules soon dispatched the crab; and Juno, unable to lessen the fame of Hercules, placed the crab which had annoyed the hero among the constellations, where it is now called Cancer.

MYTHOLOGY DICTIONARY

Hygeia - The deity of health. She was the daughter of Aesculapius.

Hymen - The son of Bacchus and Venus. He was the deity of marriage.

Hyperion - The son of Coelus and Terra. He was the father of Aurora. The poets often use his name to signify the sun.

I

Iarbas - A son of Jupiter and Garamantis. From him, Dido purchased the ground on which she built Carthage. Rather than marry larbas. Dido destroyed herself.

Incarnation – The belief that spirit takes on physical form or characteristics.

Indra - The Deity of heaven among the Hindus.

Inshushinak – Major deity of the Elamites. The ancient ziggurat of Choga Zanbil is dedicated to him.

Iris - The messenger of the Deities, but more particularly of Juno. She is the same as the rainbow.

Ishtar – Babylonian deity of war and fertility.

Isis - A celebrated deity of the Egyptians. She was often represented as the moon, and her brother Osiris as the sun.

Hygeia

Itzpapalotl – Aztec female deity that ruled over paradise.

Ixion - A king of Thessaly, who for his many perfidies was doomed by Jupiter to be tied to a wheel in hell which continually revolved.

Izangi – Creation myth deity in Japanese mythology.

MYTHOLOGY DICTIONARY

J

Jackalope – Mythical creature with a jackrabbit body and antelope antlers, featured in American folklore. Legend has it that rabbits infected with the virus cause antlers to grow on their heads.

Jade Emperor – Deity of heaven in Chinese Taoist mythology.

Janus - The son of Apollo. His temple at Rome was open in time of war^ and shut in time of peace. During a period of 700 years, it was only closed three times.

Japetus - A son of Coelus and Terra. He was regarded as the father of mankind. Hence old men frequently received the name of Japeti.

Janus

Jason - A descendant of Aeolus a celebrated hero whose education was entrusted to the centaur Chiron. He commanded the expedition to Colchis, in search of the golden fleece, which by the assistance of Medea, he triumphantly brought to Thessaly.

MYTHOLOGY DICTIONARY

Johnny Appleseed – American nurseryman credited with spreading Apple trees across America.

Jorogumo – Giant mythical spider that seduces males in Japanese culture.

Juno - Daughter of Saturn and Ops, the wife of Jupiter, the queen of all the deities, and the mistress of heaven and earth. The worship of this deity was universal among the ancients, and her sacrifices were made with equal solemnity with those of Jupiter.

Jupiter - Deity of Saturn and Ops, and the supreme deity of the ancients. Having become master of the universe by the subjugation of the Titans, he divided the empire with his brothers Neptune and Pluto, to whom he respectively gave the empires of the sea and the infernal regions, reserving for himself the kingdom of heaven.

Juventas - The Deity of youth at Rome, the same as the Hebe of the Greeks.

JUNO.

K

Kappa – Japanese water demon.

Karma – The belief that one's life course is determined based on their actions, whether good or bad. Featured in Asian cultures.

JUPITER.

Khumban – Elamite deity of the sky.

Kiririsha – Female Elamite deity.

Kodama – Japanese tree spirit.

Kuanyin, known as Kwannon

MYTHOLOGY DICTIONARY

Korrigan – Mythical dwarf like character that originated in France.

Kotoamatsukami – The first deities in the creation myth of the Shinto religion in Japan.

Kraken – Giant mythical sea monster that resembles a squid, first introduced by Norwegian sailors.

Kuanyin – Also known as Guanyin or Kwannon was a Female deity that was worshipped in Japan. Kwannon, also known as Guan Yin, came to Japan via China and was worshipped as a male deity before the 12th century. Kwannon was a Taoist deity that was imported in to Japan and took on a female form or even androgynous form. Taoists view Guanyin (Kwannon) as a male deity but it is important to note that his transformation in to a female one came about under the patriarchal Japanese culture.

Kukulkán – Mayan equivalent of Quetzalcoatl, feathered serpent.

L

Lachamee – She was the deity of plenty among the Hindus.

Lamassu – Winged bird with the body of a bull. Featured in Assyrian culture as a female protective deity.

Lamlae or Lemures – The monsters (by some supposed to be the manes of the dead), who disturbed the peace of all humankind, terrifying the good and haunting the wicked.

Lancelot – Mythical French Knight that served under King Arthur.

Lares - Household Deities among the Romans.

Latona - The mother of Apollo and Diana.

Laverna – She was the deity of thieves and dishonest persons at Rome.

Ganesha

MYTHOLOGY DICTIONARY

Lei Gong – Chinese deity of thunder.

Lemuria – 1) Feasts instituted by Romulus to appease the manes of the dead. 2) Mythical land bridge between the Pacific Ocean and the Indian Ocean.

Lethe - A river of hell, whose waters were drunk by the souls of the dead, to cause them to forget whatever they had done, seen, or heard.

Libitina – She was a deity at Rome, who presided over funerals. Persons who undertook the whole care and charge of funerals, were called Libitinarii.

Llorona – Crying woman that haunts the countryside searching for her dead drowned children after she killed them, featured in Colombian folklore.

Loch Ness Monster – Scottish folklore about a serpent like creature that lives in lake (Loch) Ness in Scotland.

MYTHOLOGY DICTIONARY

Loki – Norse deity of mischief.

Lucifer – 1) A name given by the poets to the planet Venus, when a morning star. 2) Name used by Christians to refer to Satan.

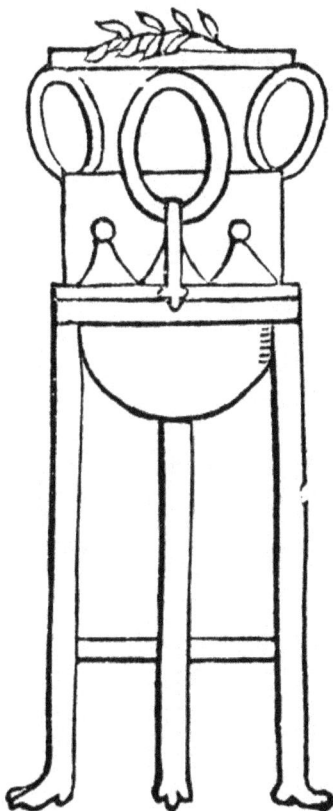

MYTHOLOGY DICTIONARY

Lugus – Deity of light in Celtic mythology.

Luna - The daughter of Hyperion and Terra. The name signifies the moon.

Lupercalia - Feasts held at Rome in honor of the deity Pan.

Lycanthropy – Disease that turned humans in to a werewolf (part human, part wolf). Humans that were afflicted with this disease were called Lycans.

Lycsia - Feasts held by the Greeks in honor of the deity Pan.

Lycurgides - Days of solemnity appointed to be kept annually in honor of Lycurgus, the great Spartan lawgiver.

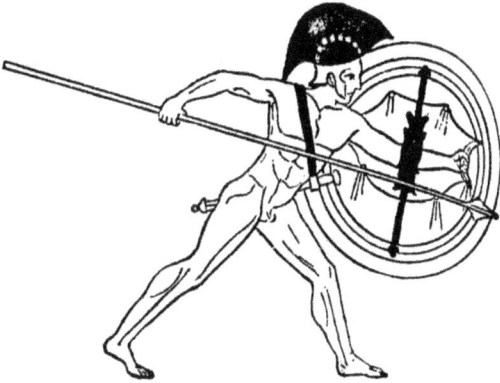

M

Macedo - A son of Osiris who gave his name to Macedonia.

Madremonte – Mother of the forest or Mother Earth in Colombian mythology.

Maenads - Surname of the Bacchantes or priestesses of Bacchus.

Magi – Iranian religious priests that attained great celebrity for their skill in mathematics, philosophy ,and astronomy.

Mama – Demon that has been known to communicate with users of the Talking Board. Mama is also known as Mimi.

Maenads

Mandingas – Satanic representation that steals humans souls in Colombian mythology.

Manes - A name applied to the souls of the dead. They were worshipped with much solemnity, particularly by the Romans.

Mania – She was a deity, represented to be the mother of the Manes and the Lares.

Marishi – Buddhist female deity associated with light.

Mars - A son of Jupiter and Juno. He was the deity of war, and was greatly reverenced by the Romans as their patron deity.

M A R S.

Mather – Cotton Mather was a Harvard trained pamphleteer that

claimed to have seen witches.
Mather is believed to be indirectly
responsible for the creation of the
Salem Witch Trials.

Mazu – Chinese deity of the sea.

Medea - A famous enchantress, the
daughter of Aeetes, King of Colchis.
She married Jason; and it was owing
entirely to her efforts that the
Argonauts succeeded in then-
enterprise.

Medium – Individual that invites a
spirit to control them in order to
speak through them.

Medusa - One of the three Gorgons.
After her head was cut off by
Perseus, it retained the power of
turning into stone all who looked
upon it so horrifying was its
appearance. This head subsequently
formed the boss of Minerva's shield.

Megaera - One of the Furies. She,
like her sisters, was deputed by the
Deities to punish mankind for their
crimes, by bringing upon them
diseases and death.

MYTHOLOGY DICTIONARY

Melpomene - One of the nine daughters of Jupiter and Mnemosyne. She presided over tragedy.

Menehune – Mythical dwarf tribe in Hawaii.

Mercurius - The son of Jupiter and Maia. He was employed by all the deities as their messenger and particularly by Jupiter, who furnished him with a winged cap called petasus and with wings for his feet called talaria, to add to his natural swiftness. Mercury was not only the deity of eloquence but also of dishonesty. To Mercury was appointed the charge of conducting the souls of the dead to their future abode. This deity was called Hermes by the Greeks.

Merlin – Druid and magician. Raised King Arthur from infanthood and served as his consultant.

Merope - One of the Atlantides. The wife of Sisyphus.

Meru - The Hindu lawgiver.

Mermaid – Female creatures that were half human and half fish with the ability enchant sailors with their exquisite beauty.

MERCURY.

Metis - One of the Oceanides. Jupiter's first wife.

Mictlan – Underworld in Aztec mythology.

Midas - A king of Phrygia, endowed by Bacchus with the power of turning every- thing he touched into gold. Being desirous afterwards of having this power taken from him (for it

threatened his destruction by
starvation), he was ordered
to bathe in the Pactolus whose
sands were thus turned into gold.
For having admired the music of
Pan, in preference to that of Apollo
the offended deity changed
the ears of Midas into those of an
ass.

Minerva – She was the deity of
wisdom, war, and the sciences. She
sprang from the brains of Jupiter, full
grown and in complete armor.

Minos – A king of Crete, he was
famed for his justice, moderation,
and the excellence of his laws. After
his death, he is represented by the
poets as presiding in the Infernal
Regions, the supreme judge of the
dead.

Mnemosyne - A daughter of Coelus
and Terra. She was the mother of
the nine Muses.

Mohana – Colombian water spirit.

Moloch – Canaanite deity
associated with child sacrifice cults.

MYTHOLOGY DICTIONARY

Momus - The deity of satire and raillery. He was expelled from heaven for satirizing the deities.

Morgana – Evil half-sister of King Arthur.

Mors - The deity of death, an infernal deity, worshipped by the ancients.

Mu – Fabled lost continent proposed by Augustus Le Plongeon.

Mula Retinta – Mule shaped creature that causes storms in Colombian mythology.

Muse - The nine daughters of Jupiter and Mnemosyne. They presided over the sciences and liberal arts. Their names were Calliope, Clio, Euterpe, Erato, Melpomene, Polyhymnia, Terpsichore, Thalia, and Urania. Calliope presided over eloquence and heroic poetry, Clio over history, Euterpe over music, Erato over poetry, lyric and amatory, Melpomene over tragedy, Polyhymnia over singing and rhetoric Terpsichore over dancing, Thalia over pastoral and comic poetry; and Urania over astronomy. They are sometimes called Pierides, from Mount Pierus, where they were born.

MINERVA.

Mut – Egyptian deity of the sky.

Muta - The deity of silence among the Romans.

MYTHOLOGY DICTIONARY

N

Naenia – She was the Deity of funerals at Rome. The funeral song, in praise of the deceased was called Naenia.

Nahundi – Elamite deity of the sun.

Naiades - Inferior deities who presided over rivers, springs, and fountains.

Napir – Elamite deity of the moon.

Necessitas - The mother of the Parcae.

Nemesis - An infernal deity the deity of revenge, always ready to punish impiety and all other crimes.

Neptunus - The Deity of the sea. He was the son of Saturn and Ops, and the brother of Jupiter, Pluto, and Juno.

Nike

NEPTUNE.

Nereides - Nymphs of the sea, fifty in number, whose duty it was to attend upon the superior deities of the sea.

Nereus - A deity of the sea. He was the father of the Nereides. The word Nereus is often used for the sea itself.

MYTHOLOGY DICTIONARY

Ninmah – Mother deity of Sumerian mythology.

Ninus - The founder of the Assyrian monarchy, B.C. 2059. After his death this king received divine honors, and became the Jupiter of the Assyrians and the Hercules of the Chaldeans.

Niobe - The daughter of Tantalus, and sister to Pelops. She ridiculed the honors paid to Latona, who in revenge, urged Apollo and Diana to slay her fourteen children. On account of this dreadful calamity, Niobe wept herself into a stone.

Nox - The daughter of Chaos and one of the most ancient of the deities. She married Erebus, and was the mother of Day and Light.

Nuwa – Chinese deity of creation.

O

Oceanides - Sea nymphs, daughters of Oceanus and Tethys.

Oceanus - The son of Coelus and Terra. He was considered a powerful deity of the sea, and was solemnly invoked by sailors before they entrusted themselves on the bosom of his empire.

Niobe

Occult – Secret or hidden knowledge.

MYTHOLOGY DICTIONARY

Ocypete - One of the Harpies. Whatever she touched she defiled.

Odin – Norse deity of healing and sorcery.

Ometeotl – Aztec deity that rules over other Aztec deities and represented as the creator of the universe.

Ops - The daughter of Coelus and Terra, wife of Saturn, and mother of Jupiter. She was the same as the Rhea of the Greeks.

Oracle – A device for forecasting the future.

Oreades - Nymphs of the mountains. They generally attended Diana when hunting.

Orgia - Festivals in honor of Bacchus.

Orpheus - The son of Apollo, who charmed even rocks, rivers, and fountains with the sound of his lyre.

Orus – Also known as Horus, the son of Osiris and Isis, an Egyptian deity.

Osiris - The supreme deity of the Egyptians. The ox was the symbol of Osiris, or the sun. He was the son of Jupiter and Niobe, and the husband and brother of Isis or the moon.

Ouija – Combination of the French "Oui" and German "Ja" words meaning "yes". The Ouija Board patent and trademark is owned by Hasbro but was created off the Spirit Board or Talking Board, which has been used to communicate with spirits.

Oya – Deity of winds and storms, worshipped in Latin America and Africa. Part of the Yoruba religion.

P

Pactolus - A river of Lydia, in which Midas washed when endowed with the power of turning into gold whatever he touched; from this circumstance the sands of the river became gold.

Paean - A hymn sung in honor of Apollo.

MYTHOLOGY DICTIONARY

Pagan – A person that believes in polytheistic religions, practices polytheism.

Pales – She was the Deity of pastures and sheepfolds.

Palilia - Feasts held in honor of Pales at Rome.

Pallas - A surname of Minerva. She acquired this name either from having slain the giant Pallas, or from the spear she held.

Pan - The deity of shepherds and hunters. His favorite residence was in Arcadia. He was a monster in appearance, having two small horns on his head, and his feet like those of a goat.

Panacea - A daughter of
Aesculapius and a deity of health.

Panathanaea – Summer festivals
held in Greece in honor of Minerva.

Pandora - A woman made of clay by
Vulcan. All the Deities endowed her
with valuable gifts, excepting Jupiter,
whose gift was a box containing all
kinds of evils. This box being opened

by her husband, the evils contained therein dispersed themselves all over the world and still continue to afflict mankind. Hope alone remained at the bottom, which still consoles the afflicted.

Panope - One of the Nereides.

Pantheon - A temple at Rome, dedicated to all the deities.

Paranormal – Phenomena that cannot be explained by modern science.

Parcae - Deity who presided over the lives of mortals. Their names were Clotho, Lachesis, and Atropos. They were supposed to spin and cut the thread of human life; hence they are represented as old women: the first holding a spindle, the second a distaff, and the third a pair of scissors.

Parthenon - A temple sacred to Minerva at Athens.

Patasola – Female seductive jungle monster in Colombian mythology.

Pax - The deity of peace.

Pegasus - A winged horse, which sprang from the blood of Medusa when slain by Perseus. Pegasus was the favorite of the Muses. Pelops, the son of Tantalus, killed by his father, to try the divinity of the Deities when they visited Phrygia, his limbs being served to them in a dish. Jupiter restored Pelops to life, and punished the cruelty of Tantalus in a remarkable manner.

Penates - Inferior deities among the

Romans. They presided over the domestic affairs of families. Their statues were made of wax, ivory, or silver, etc and were placed in the most secret parts of the dwelling.

Peripatetici - A sect of philosophers, so called from their receiving the lectures of their master (Aristotle) while walking.

Phaeton - The son of Phoebus, who asked the guidance of his father's chariot for one day, in order to publish to all the world his true origin. The horses of the sun, sensible of his inefficiency, departed from their customary track, threatening destruction to the universe; to prevent which, Jupiter hurled him from the chariot into the river Po. His body was after-wards buried by the nymphs of the place.

Phaetontides - The sisters of Phaeton, who, while mourning the unhappy end of their brother, were changed by Jupiter into poplars.

Philomela - A daughter of Pandion,

king of Athens, changed into a
nightingale.

Phlegethon - A river in hell, whose
waters were always at boiling point.

Phobos - A son of Mars and the
deity of terror.

MYTHOLOGY DICTIONARY

Phoebe - A surname of Diana or Luna, from the brightness of the moon.

Phoebus – A surname of Apollo or the sun, from the brightness of that luminary.

Phorcus - A sea deity, he was the father of the Gorgons.

Pierides - A name given to the Muses from their birthplace.

Pierus - A mountain in Thessaly, sacred to the Muses.

Pindus - A mountain, celebrated as being sacred to Apollo and the Muses.

Pitho - The daughter of Mercury and Venus, she was the deity of persuasion.

Planchette – Small triangular shaped wooden device used as a pointer on the Ouija Board.

Pleiades - A name given to the seven daughters of Atlas and

MYTHOLOGY DICTIONARY

Pleione, one of the Oceanides. They form the constellation in the heavens called Pleiades, near Taurus in the Zodiac.

Pluto - A son of Saturn and Ops. The deity of the infernal regions.

Plutus - The deity of riches. The son of Ceres.

Pollear - The son of Seeva, a Hindu divinity, represented with an elephant's head. He and many thousand inferior deities, the sons of Casayopa and Aditi, are ignorantly worshipped by the Hindus.

Pollo Maligno – Mythical bird that preys on hunters in Colombian mythology.

Pollux - The son of Jupiter. He and his twin brother Castor enjoy immortality alternately.

Polyphemus - One of the Cyclops, who dwelt on the coast of Sicily and fed upon human flesh. Ulysses killed this monster.

PLUTO.

Pomona - A deity at Rome, who presided over fruit trees.

Popol Vuh – Book of Mayan mythology that contains the Mayan creation myth.

Possession – Demonic control of a human by an evil spirit.

MYTHOLOGY DICTIONARY

Potion – Drinkable concoction that is able to give its user various powers; Strength, invincibility, healing, etc.

Priapus - A deity who protected gardens from predators: he was the son of Venus.

Progressive Entrapment – Deceptive process used by an evil spirit to control a human.

Prometheus - A son of Japetus, and the brother of Atlas, remarkable for his cunning, whereby Jupiter himself was deceived. He stole fire from the chariot of the sun, wherewith he animated figures of clay, which he had formed. To punish his audacity, Jupiter commanded him chained to Mount Caucasus for 30,000 years with a vulture gnawing his liver: Hercules released him from this painful position, and killed the vulture, thirty years afterwards.

Proserpine - The daughter of Ceres and the wife of Pluto.

MYTHOLOGY DICTIONARY

Proteus - A sea deity, the son of Oceanus. He had the power of assuming any shape he pleased.

Pseudoscience – Beliefs or claims not rooted in science.

Psyche - The wife of Cupid and deity of the mind. The word signifies the soul.

Pudicitia – She is the deity of chastity. The Romans deified this virtue.

Pyramus - A youth of Babylon, who not being allowed to marry a girl named this be agreed to meet her under a certain mulberry tree, where they killed them-selves with the same sword. Their blood dyed the fruit of the tree a deep purple, which before was white.

Q

Quirinus - A surname of Mars amongst the Romans. Romulus being the supposed son of Mars, was worshipped under this name after his mysterious death.

MYTHOLOGY DICTIONARY

Quetzalcoatl – Aztec deity of science and art, represented in the shape of a feathered serpent.

R

Ra – Egyptian deity of the sun.

Ragnarok – Underworld in Norse mythology.

Reincarnation – The belief that you will be re-born in to a new body after death.

MYTHOLOGY DICTIONARY

Remuria - Festivals at Rome instituted by Romulus, afterwards called Lemuria.

Rhadamanthus - A son of Jupiter, made a judge in hell on account of the justice and moderation he evinced while reigning a monarch upon earth.

Rhea - A daughter of Coelus and Terra. She was the wife of Saturn. She is sometimes named Ops, Cybele or Tellus. She is the mother of Jupiter, Neptune, Pluto, Juno, Vesta, and Ceres.

Romulus and Remus – Mythical founders of the city of Rome, Italy.

Rostam – Mythical warrior in Iranian folklore.

S

Sachi - The wife of Indra and queen of heaven among the Hindus.

Iris

Sage – 1) Wise man 2) Native American plant used to ward off evil spirits or negative energy.

Salus - The deity of health at Rome. She is the same as the Hygeia of the Greeks.

MYTHOLOGY DICTIONARY

Satan – Name used by Abrahamic religions (Judaism, Christianity, Islam) to refer to the Devil.

Saturnalia - Feasts in honor of Saturn. During the celebration of these festivals, the utmost joy and freedom prevailed. All enmities ceased, and slaves and freemen mingled in the same conviviality, in commemoration of the happy state of man during the golden reign of Saturn.

Saturnia - A name given to Juno, as being the daughter of Saturn.

Saturnius - A name applied to Jupiter, Pluto, and Neptune, as sons of Saturn.

Saturnus - A son of Coelus and Terra, the Deity of time. He devoured his male children as soon as they were born. His wife, however, contrived to save Jupiter, Pluto, and Neptune. It was usual to sacrifice human victims upon his altar. Saturn reigned some time in Italy, and

under his administration mankind
were happy, that his reign is termed
the Golden Age.

Satyri - Represented in the
form of men, but covered with hair,
and having their feet and legs like
goats, and short horns on their head.
They are the same as the Fauns.

Séance - Ritual used to contact a
spirit of the dead.

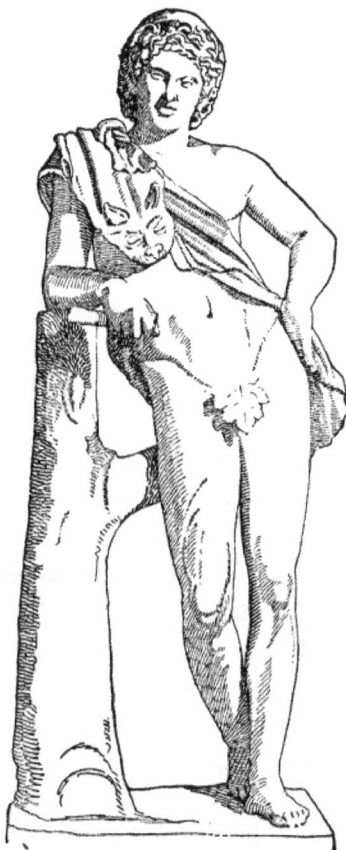

Seeva - A Hindu deity, supposed to be the destroyer of all animal and vegetable creation. His temple at Juggernaut is annually the resort of many hundred thousand pilgrims. Under the form of a bull this deity is drawn on a car in procession, when his most devoted worshippers throw themselves on the ground, to be crushed under the wheels.

Semele - A grand-daughter of Mars and Venus, and the mother of the Deity Bacchus.

Semones - A name given to the inferior deities, as Pan, the Satyrs, Priapus, Janus.

Semiramis – Mesopotamian female deity.

Septerion - A festival observed every nine years at Delphi in honor of Apollo.

Serapis - An ancient Egyptian deity, supposed to be the same as the bull Apis. A magnificent temple was dedicated to him at Alexandria.

Seshanaga - The king of the infernal regions among the Hindus. He is represented as having a thousand heads, and on each a crown of sparkling gems. Seshanaga is also the king of serpents.

Seth – Egyptian deity of disorder.

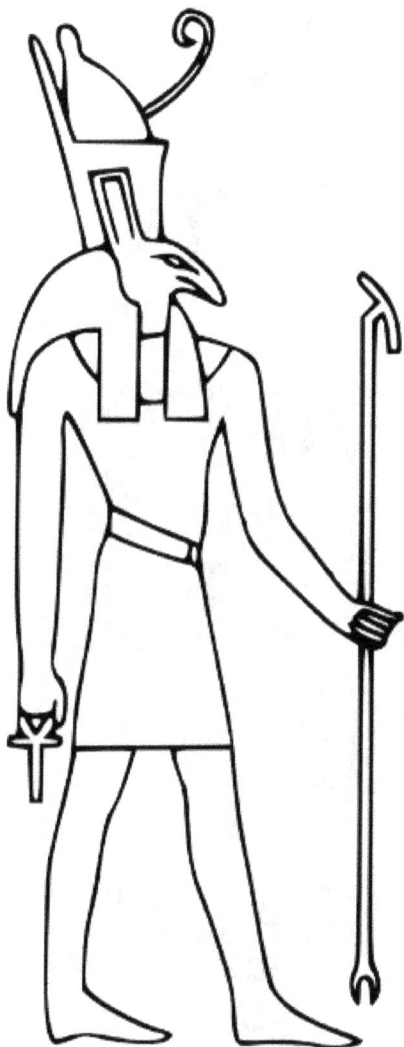

Sol

Soothsayer

Sewer Alligator – Urban legend that rose in 1920's New York, about a man eating alligator that lived and moved through the sewer system.

MYTHOLOGY DICTIONARY

Shahnama – The longest poem written by a single human. Epic poem with 50,000 couplets. Written by Ferdowsi, based on Iranian mythology and folklore.

Shichi-fuku-jin – Seven Deities of Luck in Japanese mythology.

Sibyllae - Women who pretended to be inspired by heaven to foretell future events. Sibyls have flourished, at different periods, in different parts of the earth.

Side - The wife of Orion, thrown into the infernal regions by Juno, for having boasted that her beauty surpassed that of the queen of heaven.

Silbon – Evil murderous spirit that carries a sack of bones in Colombian and Venezuelan folklore.

Silenus - The foster father of the Deity Bacchus, esteemed a demi-Deity. He had a temple dedicated to him at Elis. Silenus accompanied Bacchus in his eastern expedition; and it was for having befriended

MYTHOLOGY DICTIONARY

Silenus (who had lost his way in Phrygia) that Midas was rewarded by Bacchus with the power of turning every thing he touched into gold.

Silvanus - A rural deity. He presided over gardens and boundaries.

Simorgh – Mythical bird in Iranian mythology. Has a human face with a peacock body and lion claws. The Simorgh's size was said to have been that of 30 birds.

Sisyphus - The son of Aeolus, doomed to roll a huge stone up a mountain in hell, which continually rolled back; thus his punishment was perpetual. This rigorous sentence he received, on account of his numerous perfidies.

Smintheus - A surname of Apollo in Phrygia, where he had a temple.

Sobek – Egyptian deity of fertility and war.

Socrates - An illustrious Athenian philosopher who was endowed by nature with a sound judgment and great fortitude of mind, he early discovered the errors of the religion in which he had been educated, and conscientiously devoted himself to the instruction and enlightenment of the youth of Athens. He taught the immortality of the soul, the almighty power of the Creator of the universe, the certainty of future rewards and punishments, and the necessity of a virtuous life. He was brought to trial charged with bringing the worship of the Deities into contempt, and condemned to death. His wisdom and exemplary life made a deep impression on his countrymen, who, after his death, revered his memory and punished his accusers. The doctrines of Socrates raised the moral tone of the Athenian character, and laid the foundation of the sects of the Platonists, Stoics, Peripatetics, Academics, Cyrenaics which subsequently arose.

Sohrab – Mythical leader of Turanian army (Turkish) featured in Iranian folklore.

Sol - The sun; worshipped by the Persians under the name of Mithras, by the Chaldeans under that of Baal or Bel, by the Canaanites under that of Moloch, by the Syrians under that of Adonis, and by the Egyptians under that of Osiris. Sol, Apollo, and Phoebus are supposed to be the same deity.

Somnus - The Deity of sleep. He was the son of Erebus and Nox.

Soothsayer – Ancient fortune-teller.

Soucouyant – Black female Vampire myth prominent in Caribbean cultures.

Spell – Incantation written or spoken in order to effect, change, or control a physical object (animate or inanimate).

Spiritualist – A person that uses methods such as Automatic Writing, the Ouija Board, Séances, etc. to communicate with the dead or supernatural forces.

Stentor - A Greek, whose voice was louder than that of fifty men together.

Stheno - One of the Gorgons.

Stoici - A sect of philosophers founded by Zeno of Citium.

Styx - A river of hell, held in such

veneration, that when the Deities swore by it, their oath was irrevocable.

Suada - The deity of persuasion among the Romans. She is the same as the Pitho of the Greeks.

Susano – Japanese deity of the seas.

Sylvanus - The deity of woods.

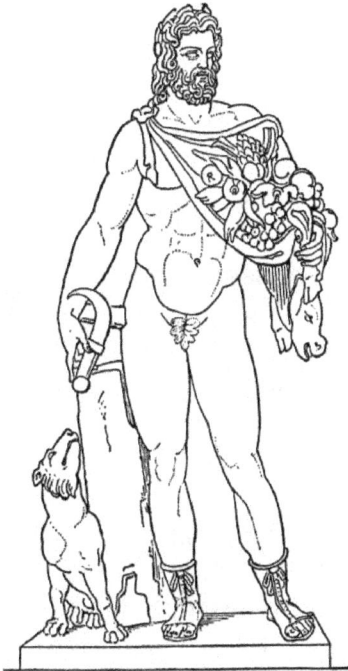

MYTHOLOGY DICTIONARY

Syrens - Three sea nymphs, daughters of Achelous and the Muse Calliope. Their names were Parthenope, Ligeia, and Leucosia. They charmed people with the sweetness of their voice, and then devoured them. Ulysses, to protect himself from their enchantment, while sailing past that part of the coast of Sicily inhabited by them, caused himself to be tied to the mast of his ship and the ears of the ship's crew to be shut.

T

Talos – Protector of Crete and Europa, had a body of bronze.

Tam Kung – Chinese sea deity.

Tantalus - A son of Jupiter, and the father of Niobe and Pelops. To try the divinity of the Deities, he killed Pelops, and served up his limbs in a dish : for which wickedness he was plunged up to the chin in a lake of hell, whose waters escaped from his lips, whenever he attempted to drink; at the same time a tree, laden with delicious fruit, hung over his head, whose branches swung from his grasp whenever he attempted to seize them. Thus, with food and drink apparently within his reach, he was doomed to suffer perpetual hunger and thirst.

Taranis – Deity of thunder in Celtic mythology.

Tarasque – Mythical creature that was a cross between a turtle and a dragon, featured in French folklore.

Tartarus - That region of hell to which were banished those of the dead who were adjudged to have been the most wicked and impious in their lives. Here Ixion, Sisyphus, Tityus suffered punishment.

Talisman – Object embedded with a spell or spells giving it supernatural power.

Talking Board – Spirit Board also known as Ouija Board.

Tao – Dualistic belief that forces of good and evil balance each other out, featured in Chinese culture.

Telepathy – Transmission of information without physical interaction.

Tempe - A beautiful vale of Thessaly, between mounts Olympus and Ossa.

Teoyaomiqui – Aztec deity of flowers.

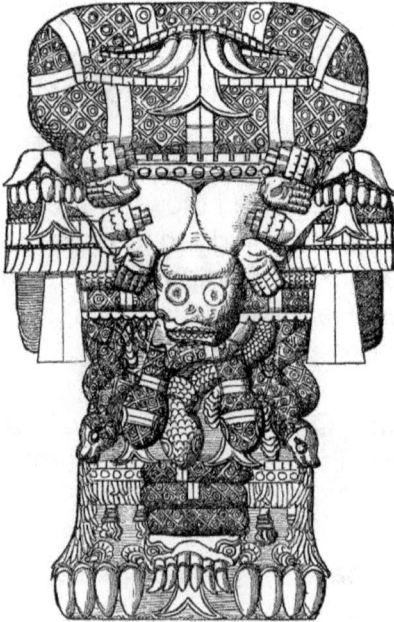

Terminalia - Festivals at Rome in honor of the Deity Terminus.

MYTHOLOGY DICTIONARY

Terminus - The Deity of boundaries.

Terpsichore - One of the Muses. She presided over dancing.

Terra - She was the wife of Uranus, and the mother of the Titans, Giants, Cyclops, etc.

Tethys - A sea deity, the wife of Oceanus, and the daughter of Uranus and Terra. She was the mother of all the chief rivers of the world, and of about 3000 daughters called Oceanides.

Teutas - The name of Mercury among the Gauls.

Tezcatlipoca – Aztec deity of time and deity of the sky.

Thalia - One of the Muses. She pre-sided over comedy and pastoral poetry.

Thea - A daughter of Uranus and Terra. She was the wife of Hyperion, and the mother of the sun and moon. She is sometimes called Rhea and Titiea.

Themis - The mother of the Parcse and of the Horae.

MYTHOLOGY DICTIONARY

Theophania - Festivals at Delphi, in honor of Apollo.

Thesmophoria - Festivals in honor of Ceres, celebrated in all the Grecian cities, but especially at Athens.

Thetis - A sea deity, the grand-daughter of Tethys, and the mother of Achilles. It was at the marriage of Thetis with ' Peleus, that the Deity of discord threw into the assemblage of divinities, who honored the ceremony with their presence, the golden apple inscribed " to the fairest of the Deities".

Thor - A Saxon deity, with the attributes of Jupiter.

Thoth - An Egyptian deity of the moon, with the attributes of Mercury.

Tiamat – Deity of creation in Babylonian mythology.

Tisiphone - One of the Furies.

Titanes - The sons of Coelus and Terra of gigantic stature and prodigious strength. They carried on a successful war against Saturn, which is much celebrated.

Titanides - The daughters of Coelus and Terra. Six in number.

Titanus - The eldest of the sons of

MYTHOLOGY DICTIONARY

Coelus and Terra, brother to Saturn, Hyperion, and Titanus. By the assistance of his brothers, vanquished Saturn, and kept him a prisoner until he was released by his son Jupiter.

Tityus - A giant said to have occupied nine acres of ground when stretched out to his full length. Apollo and Diana killed him with their arrows, and after death he was placed in Tartarus, where a serpent continually gnawed his liver.

Tlaloc – The deity of Rain in the Aztec religion.

Toutatis – French deity of protection.

Triton - A sea deity, the son of Neptune and Amphitrite, employed as his father's trumpeter. Many of the sea deities are called Tritons.

Trophonius - A man honored as a deity. He delivered oracles in a gloomy cave.

Tudigong – Chinese deity of the soil.

MYTHOLOGY DICTIONARY

Tunda – Female vampire monster in Colombian mythology.

U

Unicorn – Winged horse with supernatural abilities such as flying.

Urania - One of the Muses: she presided over astronomy.

Uranus - The most ancient of all the deities. He is the same as Coelus, and married Terra, or the earth.

Urban Legend – Modern folklore based around strange events and strange happenings such as random disappearances and tragedies. Usually rooted in local culture and is unique to the area in which it was created.

V

Vacuna - The deity of repose and leisure.

Valhalla – Mythical heaven ruled over by Odin in Norse mythology.

Vampires – Folklore based on the real life Count Dracula, about nocturnal humans that feast on the blood of humans. Their fangs can suck blood from their victims as well as turn a victim in to a vampire.

Venus - The deity of beauty. She arose from the froth of the sea, near the island of Cythera. She contested with Juno and Pallas for the apple of discord, and gained the prize. She was married to Vulcan, who was both ugly and deformed.

MYTHOLOGY DICTIONARY

Venti - The winds which were invoked by the ancients as deities. The four chief winds were Eurus, Auster, Zephyrus, and Boreas.

Vertumnus - The deity of spring. A Roman deity.

Vesper - The poetical name for the planet Venus when she shines in the evening.

Vesta - The deity of fire. She was the daughter of Saturn and Khea, and sister to Ceres and Juno. In her temple at Rome, virgins of the most noble families constantly kept the sacred fire burning on her altars.

VESTA.

Vestales - Priestesses consecrated to the service of the deity Vesta at Rome. They enjoyed great honors and privileges, but punished with death if convicted of having broken their vows. Plebeians were eligible to fill the office, if of good family and of great beauty.

Victoria - The deity of victory at Rome: By the Greeks she was called Nice.

Virtutes - All the virtues, as honor, prudence, justice, temperance, modesty, clemency, devotion, tranquility, and health, were honored as deities by the Romans.

Vishnu - A Deity of the Hindus, supposed to preserve all animal and vegetable creation.

Volumnus and Volumna - Two deities, who presided over the will, chiefly invoked to preserve concord.

MYTHOLOGY DICTIONARY

Voluptas - The deity of pleasure worshipped at Rome.

Voodoo – Tribal magic of African origin practiced by slaves in North America.

Vulcaneus - The deity of fire, famed for his deformity. He was the son of Jupiter and Juno and the husband of Venus. For interfering in the quarrels between Jupiter and Juno, he was kicked out of heaven, when he broke his leg by the fall. The Cyclops were his attendants, and with their assistance, he forged the thunderbolts of Jupiter, and fabricated arms for deities and heroes.

VULCAN.

W

Wenchang Wang – Chinese deity of culture and literature.

Wendingo – Native American myth about a flesh eating hybrid creature that ate humans.

Werewolf – Mythical creature that is a human with the ability to transform in to a wolf. Famous as a legend in Europe during the Middle Ages. Werewolves are said to be inflicted with lycanthropy, from having been bit by a wolf.

MYTHOLOGY DICTIONARY

Wicca – Pagan religion centered around the use of witchcraft.

Willow of the Wisp – Atmospheric light seen over bodies of water, attributed to supernatural forces.

Witch – A pagan that uses spells and conjuring to affect their environment.

Witchcraft – The use of spells to affect the natural environment.

Woden - A Saxon deity, with the attributes of Mars.

X

Xanthe - One of the Oceanides.

Xihe – Chinese deity of the sun.

Y

Yamen - The judge of departed spirits, among the Hindus. If the soul be considered unworthy to enter Swerga, the first heaven, it is either sent down to the region of serpents, or made to return again to earth, under some new form, either animal, vegetable, or mineral.

Yanluowang – Chinese deity of death.

Yemoja – Feminine energy force in Yoruba religion, practiced in Latin America and Africa. Controls water.

Z

Zahak – Evil figure in Iranian mythology, had snakes growing from his shoulders and engaged in cannibalism.

Zephtrus - The son of Astreus and Aurora. His name is poetically used for the west wind.

Zeno - The founder of the sect called Stoics, so called from the name of the portico at Athens, where he delivered his lectures.

Zeus - A name of Jupiter among the Greeks, as father of mankind, and the deity by whom all things are sustained.

MYTHOLOGY DICTIONARY

Zhurong – Chinese deity of fire.

Zilant – Mythical bird in Russian folklore that resembles a Dragon.

Zombies – Undead creatures that are neither dead nor alive. Haitian myths about Zombies are rampant with the most prevalent being their use as slaves that answer to the master that used Voodoo to make them a zombie.

Zozo – Ancient Babylonian demon. Also known as Pazuzu.

MYTHOLOGY DICTIONARY

OBSERVATIONS

1. Various cultures share similar beliefs.

2. Certain myths are universal among all cultures.

3. Heroes do not always win, but their defeats teach us.

4. Most folklore contains wisdom for the reader.

5. Myths are not always true, but they contain truth within them.

6. Some myths cannot be explained.

7. Many myths are fables in a story form.

8. Myths live on forever because they contain ideals and values that are common to all peoples.

MYTHOLOGY DICTIONARY

NOTES

MYTHOLOGY DICTIONARY

NOTES

NOTES

MYTHOLOGY DICTIONARY

NOTES

MYTHOLOGY DICTIONARY

NOTES

MYTHOLOGY DICTIONARY

NOTES

MYTHOLOGY DICTIONARY

NOTES

MYTHOLOGY DICTIONARY

NOTES

MYTHOLOGY DICTIONARY

NOTES

MYTHOLOGY DICTIONARY

NOTES

NOTES

MYTHOLOGY DICTIONARY

NOTES

MYTHOLOGY DICTIONARY

MIKAZUKI PUBLISHING HOUSE™
(U.S.P.T.O. Serial Number 85705702)

1) 25 Principles of Martial Arts
2) 25 Principles of Strategy
3) American Antifa
4) Arctic Black Gold
5) Art of War
6) Back to Gold
7) Basketball Team Play Design Book
8) Beginner's Magicians Manual
9) Boxing Coloring Book
10) California's Next Century 2.0
11) Camping Survival Handbook
12) Captain Bligh's Voyage
13) Coming to America Handbook
14) Customer Sales Organizer
15) DIY Comic Book
16) DIY Comic Book Part II
17) Economic Collapse Survival Manual
18) Find The Ideal Husband
19) Football Play Design Book
20) Freakshow Los Angeles
21) Game Creation Manual
22) George Washington's Farewell Address
23) Hagakure
24) History of Aliens
25) I Dream in Haiku
26) Internet Connected World

MYTHOLOGY DICTIONARY

27) Irish Republican Army Manual of Guerrilla Warfare
28) Japan History Coloring Book
29) John Locke's 2nd Treatise on Civil Government
30) Karate 360
31) Learning Magic
32) Living the Pirate Code
33) Magic as Science and Religion
34) Magicians Coloring Book
35) Make Racists Afraid Again
36) Master Password Organizer Handbook
37) Mikazuki Jujitsu Manual
38) Mikazuki Political Science Manual
39) MMA Coloring Book
40) MMA Dictionary
41) Mythology Coloring Book
42) Mythology Dictionary
43) Native Americana
44) Ninja Style
45) Ouija Board Enigma
46) Palloncino
47) Political Advertising Manual
48) Quotes Gone Wild
49) Rappers Rhyme Book
50) Self-Examination Diary
51) Shogun X the Last Immortal
52) Small Arms & Deep Pockets

MYTHOLOGY DICTIONARY

If the Mikazuki Publishing House™ book is not available, place a request with any bookstore to order it for you.
Instagram.com/MikazukiPublishingHouse

MYTHOLOGY DICTIONARY

KAMBIZ MOSTOFIZADEH TITLES
1. Mikazuki Jujitsu Manual
2. 25 Principles of Martial Arts
3. Karate 360
4. Magic as Science & Religion
5. Political Advertising Manual
6. Small Arms & Deep Pockets
7. World War Water
8. The Bribe Vibe
9. Arctic Black Gold
10. Find the Ideal Husband
11. Learning Magic
12. Mikazuki Political Science Manual
13. Van Carlton Detective Agency: Burgundy Diamond
14. Camping Survival Handbook
15. Game Creation Manual
16. Internet Connected World
17. Economic Collapse Survival Manual
18. Native Americana
19. Back To Gold
20. History of Aliens
21. Ouija Board Enigma
22. American Antifa
23. Make Racists Afraid Again
24. Mythology Dictionary
25. Ninja Style
26. MMA Dictionary
27. The Whore Knows

Facebook.com/KambizMostofizadeh
Instagram.com/KambizMostofizadeh

www.ingramcontent.com/pod-product-compliance
Lightning Source LLC
Chambersburg PA
CBHW050124280326
41933CB00010B/1237